Flower Arranging

The Winterthur Way

Alberta A. Melloy

With an Introduction by Maggie Lidz

A WINTERTHUR BOOK
DISTRIBUTED BY UNIVERSITY PRESS OF NEW ENGLAND

CREDITS

Editor: Onie Rollins
Designer: Suzanne DeMott Gaadt, Gaadt Perspectives, LLC
Printer: CS Graphics PTE LTD, Singapore
Photo credits: Laszlo Bodo: cover, ii, 51–53; Herb Crossan: 24–46, 54–66;
Gottlieb Hampfler: vi; Hagley Museum and Library: 7, 10, 12; Nemours Foundation: 4;
Peter Pagan: 21; all others courtesy Winterthur.
Quoted material: Denise Magnani et al., *The Winterthur Garden: Henry Francis du Pont's
Romance with the Land* (New York: Harry N. Abrams in assoc. with Henry Francis du Pont
Winterthur Museum, 1995): 33; all du Pont material courtesy Winterthur Archives and
Hagley Museum and Library.

Library of Congress Cataloging-in-Publication Data

Melloy, Alberta A., 1935-
  Flower arranging the Winterthur way / Alberta A.
Melloy ; with an
introduction by Maggie Lidz.
    p. cm. -- (A Winterthur book)
  ISBN 0-912724-60-9
 1. Flower arrangement. 2. Henry Francis du Pont Winterthur
Museum.
I. Henry Francis du Pont Winterthur Museum. II. Title.
 SB449 .M46 2002
 745.92--dc21
                        2002007713

Contents

Dedication

HENRY FRANCIS DU PONT, THE FOUNDER of Winterthur Museum, was a lover of nature. This book is a tribute to him and to all who appreciate the beauty and smells of nature, the seeing and feeling of it all—the wonderful surprises of spring when crocus and snowdrops pop through the cold crust of earth . . . the lovely summer field flowers that fill the meadows with "those weeds" . . . the bright reds and golds of fall foliage . . . the silhouettes of bare trees and shrubs in their nakedness, amazing the eye with their simplicity of form . . . and the cold, snowy landscape of winter that blankets and outlines the rolling hills and vistas. That is nature, and that is Winterthur.

As you go through the pages of this book, I hope that you learn about flower arranging . . . but more important, that you enjoy the beauty and splendor of Winterthur and share in this tribute to Henry Francis du Pont.

Portrait of H. F. du Pont by Aaron Shikler, 1965.

Foreword

WINTERTHUR IS A UNIQUE NATIONAL TREASURE. A du Pont family country estate in Delaware's scenic Brandywine Valley, Winterthur offers a rare combination of beauty, history, art, and learning. The museum collection of early American decorative arts remains without equal. The brilliantly conceived naturalistic garden is set amid a rolling landscape of quiet grandeur. The research library serves as an important center for the study of American art and culture.

Winterthur's floral legacy is not to be denied. It forms an integral part of the country estate tradition. Whether inside or out, the cultivation and enjoyment of nature's bounty has been of utmost importance to the generations of du Ponts who called the estate home—from the initial development of the property by Jacques Antoine and Evelina du Pont Bidermann in the mid 1800s to its full flowering under the watchful eye of Henry Francis du Pont in the 1900s.

The pages ahead tell the story. Colorful blooms that herald the change of seasons are to be found in abundance, not only outside in the garden but inside as well, in marvelous fresh arrangements, on textiles and wallpaper, and as decorative embellishments on objects ranging from porcelain to silver.

We invite you to share in our enjoyment at presenting this first-ever publication on flower arranging at Winterthur. Discover the history, admire the beauty, and learn how to create. Read on and be thrilled!

Leslie Greene Bowman
Director
Winterthur, An American Country Estate

Reflecting Pool at Winterthur.

Preface

HENRY FRANCIS DU PONT WAS A GENTLEMAN of numerous special interests. He was an extraordinary collector, horticulturist, and farmer. As a collector he was considered one of the best. He began acquiring American decorative arts in the 1920s, searching for the finest, the rarest, or a key piece that would showcase the skills of American craftsmen. He once stated, "It is fortunate that I seem to notice everything that is attractive and beautiful." The Winterthur collection contains some of the most superb examples of American architecture and decorative arts in the world.

As a horticulturist, Mr. du Pont was also one of the best, collecting rare and unusual specimens. I view him as an artist painting the landscape, adding color and texture where needed, taking advantage of the hills and vistas. The natural landscape was the dominating force in the organization and arrangement of his garden. H. F. du Pont carefully studied plant material suitable for the environment. Color, growth habit, size, and shape were considered before being introduced. The garden at Winterthur is a bold profusion of color. Over a period of some sixty years Mr. du Pont created one of the finest naturalistic gardens in the English landscape style.

Spring daffodils cover the Winterthur landscape.

My days at Winterthur as a guide specialist (1973–83) were spent studying and appreciating the vast collection of American decorative arts Henry Francis du Pont brought together in the 175 period rooms of his country estate. When I became the head flower arranger, serving from 1983 to 1990, my ambition was to combine my particular interests: providing bouquets equal to the splendor of the museum rooms. The arrangements within this book reflect what I accomplished during that period. I credit my flower arranging skills to "playing" with all sorts of plant material. My fondness for flowers mirrors that of H. F. du Pont, who commented, " I have always loved flowers and had a garden as a child . . . and if you have grown up with flowers and really seen them, you can't help to have unconsciously absorbed an appreciation of proportion, color, detail, and material."

The importance of flowers within the rooms at Winterthur is best described in Mr. du Pont's memorandum to the executors of his estate, "I shall want the spirit of the house maintained as if someone were living in it, and in order to carry this out I shall want among other things, flowers kept in certain vases in certain rooms." His intention was to bring the "outdoor" color of the garden to the "indoor" museum rooms.

When H. F. du Pont and his wife, Ruth, resided at Winterthur, there often were as many as ten or twenty bouquets in a room. The flowers came from specialized cutting gardens and

greenhouses that contained walk-in refrigerators to preserve the blossoms. His lush arrangements were of one variety and one color using massive punch bowls, soup tureens, and vases. He also liked displaying a single specimen in a bud vase. Ten bouquets in a room could make one feel overcome, but with one flower type and one color, everything blended to make a total picture. The Chinese Parlor, seen here, shows a number of bouquets done in the manner of H. F. du Pont.

Chinese Parlor.

Branches of quince, pale pink stock, and sweet peas and a bud vase with white freesia fill the room. The color and scale are in balance and mesh perfectly.

Color was more than important to H. F. du Pont; it was the key element. The daily color range of flowers available dictated his selection of table services for his dining room. Mr. du Pont's daughter Ruth du Pont Lord tells us that "my father alone was in charge of the dining room, and he approached it as if he were designing a stage set. His material—flowers, china, linen—was assembled in advance, the availability of flowers determining the other choices. Three or four days before a house party, a gardener would bring him samples of outdoor or greenhouse flowers that

Preface

could be counted on to be blooming. (A flower to be used on the table was not to be seen anywhere else in the house that day.) My father and the butler would then decide on the combination of china, glass, and linen that would best complement the flowers." Like the menus, lists of flowers and their containers for the dining room were recorded for sixty years (from 1908 to 1968). Also recorded for a period of fifty-eight years, beginning in 1910, are the day-by-day combinations of flowers, china, and linen that appeared on the Winterthur table.

The floral arrangements at Winterthur today are of a mixed variety, with a lesser number on display. They are planned with color in mind, blending with the window hangings, upholstery, wall coverings, paintings, and rugs. The containers reflect the style period of the rooms in which they are placed.

When I was asked by former director Thomas A. Graves Jr. to write this book, I was, of course, extremely pleased but a bit overwhelmed with a deep sense of responsibility. For beautiful bouquets have always had a special place at Winterthur. They will forever be part of the du Pont legacy.

It has truly been my privilege and honor to take part in that legacy and to present these bouquets for the many readers who are about to experience the incomparable beauty and majesty of Winterthur's way with flowers.

Acknowledgments

IT IS WITH APPRECIATION AND MUCH GRATITUDE that I acknowledge the special people who helped me through the pages of *Flower Arranging the Winterthur Way:* Thomas A. Graves Jr., former Director of Winterthur, who invited me to write the book; Gary Kulik, Deputy Director for Library, Collections Management, and Academic Programs, for his continued encouragement; Onie Rollins, Susan Randolph, and Teresa Vivolo, Publications Department, for their editorial expertise; Herb Crossan and Laszlo Bodo, for their beautiful photography; Suzanne Gaadt for her exquisite design; Ruth Joyce, for her horticultural assistance with the glossary; and Patty Pleva, Marlin Dise, and all the garden staff and volunteers who grew and cut the hundreds of beautiful flowers and plant material for our arrangements.

Particular thanks to the "flower ladies" who lovingly helped me arrange the luscious bouquets in the flower room: Joanne Deaton, Tala Graham, Bea Edgar, Ann Jacobs, Gail Lam, Biddie Mearns, Isabella Tarumianz, Ellen Whitaker, Bonnie Beck, Nancy Bowman, and Betty Ann Brose. And a special debt of gratitude to Iris Coggins, who was at my side throughout the final stages of the book.

A most sincere thanks as well to my husband, Joe, for always being supportive and truly my best friend.

Maggie Lidz

In the Beginning...

BEFORE BUILDING THE HOUSE AT WINTERTHUR, planning its garden, or even siting the well, Evelina du Pont Bidermann and her husband, Jacques Antoine, the first owners of the estate, considered flowers. While visiting France in 1838, a year before construction began on their home in Delaware, Evelina (the great-aunt of H. F. du Pont) wrote to her sister, "Antoine . . . is getting a plan here for our House in which he has not forgotten the little Greenhouse, if such may be termed a little room for flowers."

Evelina's passion was flowers. The same can be said of each subsequent owner of Winterthur— gardeners all. And "flower arranging is," as stated

Fragrant lilacs, a favorite of H. F. du Pont, grace his 1914 portrait by Ellen Emmet Rand.

The museum is seen through the lush ground cover of ferns and azaleas.

Introduction

in Gertrude Jekyll's 1907 *Flower Decoration in the House,* "a branch of gardening." The second mistress of Winterthur, Pauline Foster du Pont, was so fond of flowers that for decades after her death she was remembered for her generosity in giving away endless bouquets of lilies. Her son, Henry Francis du Pont, the third owner of Winterthur and founder of the museum, achieved national renown for his naturalistic garden and bowerlike rooms. Today the museum follows, as much as possible, the flower pattern set by the private home. In all the main reception rooms, flowers are replenished twice a week. They are stored and arranged in the special "flower-fixing" room with an adjacent walk-in cooler built for that purpose by H. F. du Pont in 1929. A special staff devotes many hours to the care of the weekly bouquets.

The type of floral arrangements seen at Winterthur has changed over the years. The Bidermanns, the du Ponts, and later the museum have kept up with fashion. Flowers have varied from hothouse exotics to roadside weeds, sometimes bought, sometimes found wild, many specially grown. The flowers have been gathered in modest bunches, massed to overflowing, and arranged in dramatic, single-stem displays as well. For more than one hundred and fifty years, flowers have been ornamenting the rooms at Winterthur, where the floral tradition begun by Antoine and Evelina Bidermann in 1838 carries on to this day.

Flowers from Eleuthera du Pont's scrapbook.

Evelina Bidermann and Mid-Victorian Flower Madness

ALMOST ALL REMAINING RELICS of Evelina Bidermann's life relate to her involvement with flowers: a French architectural plan depicting a house wreathed in a garden; an amethyst glass vase; a botanical scrapbook; and hundreds of letters blooming with references to flowers. Evelina's family and friends were kept up-to-date on her plant acquisitions, the state of her greenhouses and garden, and the bouquets and nosegays (her "bunches") that she cherished.

Evelina shared her hobby with her sisters: Victorine, Eleuthera, and Sophie du Pont. The women lived within ten miles of one another in the Brandywine Valley and were constantly trading plants, seeds, bulbs, and advice. Birthdays, special occasions, and trying times were celebrated and marked with flowers.

Although ribbon arrangements (flowers gathered in strands of contrasting color) and free-hanging garlands were popular in their lifetime, Evelina and her family seemed to prefer simple bouquets of homegrown varieties or wildflowers. These bouquets were loosed casually into a container and admired more as pretty garden bounty than artistic creations. Flower bunches were a natural part of the du Pont sisters' lives and punctuated the seasons of the year: hyacinths and

Introduction

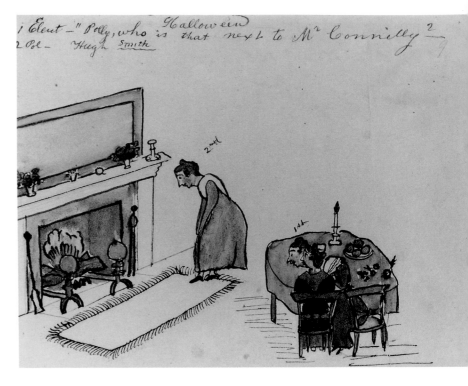

lilacs in the spring, dahlias and roses in the summer, chrysanthemums and asters in the fall, and violets and exotics through the winter.

The home in which the girls were raised, Eleutherian Mills (now part of Hagley Museum), had a large flower garden. In a humorous 1830 sketch, Sophie observed that the mantel in the parlor was "always graced by a glass containing flowers, either fresh or faded, but more frequently the latter."

The du Pont sisters' infatuation with flowers was typical for the first half of the nineteenth century, when the international enthusiasm for flowers was so intense that historians have called it "floral-mania." Almost every house was adorned with flower beds. Every imaginable surface inside was bedecked with fresh, dried, artificial, painted, embroidered, or printed flowers.

Floral-mania flourished at that time for several reasons. Technological advances of the nineteenth century changed the way people inhabited their homes. With improved heating methods, rooms became warmer, and with improved glass manufacturing processes, windows became larger. With more light and warmth, tender plants could be kept alive all winter.

This whimsical sketch by Sophie du Pont indicates the fashion for placing flowers on the mantel, 1830.

As at Eleutherian Mills, vases of fresh flowers were usually showcased on the parlor mantel. That custom would linger, but a new mode of flower arranging emerged in the 1830s. The style was seen first in France and included much extravagance.

The first full-fledged florist shop, named for proprietor Jules Lachaume, opened in Paris in 1840. Before that, flowers were sold by roving street vendors, in market stalls, or as a side business in shops devoted to other merchandise. A floral shop made life much easier for professional decorators trying to create the room-encasing, floral "compositions" demanded by the Parisian elite. Though the floor-to-ceiling flower rooms were designed for grand private entertainment, Lachaume helped spread the fashion to a wider audience. His displays were sometimes adapted to conservatory arrangements. In a May 1838 letter to her sisters, Evelina described a fashionable Parisian conservatory:

> *a colonnade of pillars round which innumerable scarce flowers twine . . . creepers and shrubs in full bloom, white, purple Azaleas, Rhododendrons . . . the tree peony & many others. The greenhouse glass all around, with, at the top, some panes of stained glass which produce a beautiful effect.*

An 1815 porcelain jar in the Winterthur collection showing the current vogue for "floral-mania."

Introduction

Drawing from an 1837 publication in the Winterthur Library illustrating the latest French designs for the floral decoration of a garden pavilion.

When Antoine and Evelina returned to America in April 1839, they must have been brimming with ideas for their new home, which they intended to call Winterthur after Antoine's ancestral town in Switzerland. They brought back bulbs and seeds, agricultural books, and architectural plans. The rest of their lives would be occupied with the development of the Winterthur estate. Until her death in 1863, Evelina worked on the garden, creating beds of roses, asters, and dahlias; arranging a heated greenhouse for winter blooms; and overseeing the management of a forcing shed for early spring flowers.

The architectural plans Evelina and Antoine carried from France hang today in Winterthur's Memorial Library, a room named in honor of past residents of the estate. The drawings seem to have been used more as a suggestion than a line-for-line model for the Bidermanns' country house in Delaware. The garden-side gallery was adopted and remained in place through 1902. Open in the

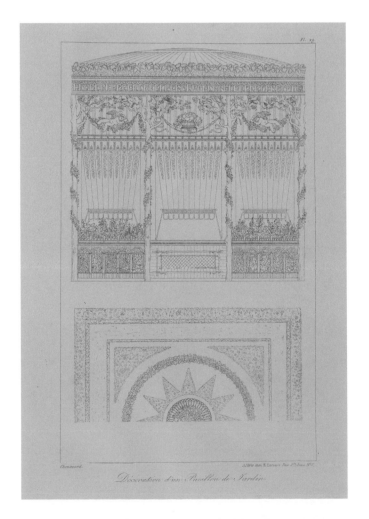

*Architectural plan made for Jacques Antoine and
Evelina du Pont Bidermann in France, 1838.*

summer and glassed-in and heated during the winter, this back porch functioned as Evelina's "flower room."

Each year from October to May, Evelina tended her scent-filled indoor garden. A wealth of plants flourished: a bay laurel tree, a rhododendron, two lemon trees, a fragrant daphne, roses, white camellias, azaleas, a night-blooming cereus vine, mignonette, dahlias, primroses, cinerarias, geraniums, and two types of violets. The sweet Parma violets, "double white in bloom, mixed they make beautiful bunches," were especially prized.

On winter evenings, Evelina and Antoine took after-dinner strolls in their "fairy palace." During the spring, they walked in the outside garden, which was filled with lilies of the valley, yellow violets, white anemones, hyacinths, hepatica, primroses, jonquils, and lilacs. Behind the house, Evelina planted a circle of ten ever-blooming rose bushes. She often mixed those roses with "daisy

*An 1883 summer view of the Winterthur house showing the
back porch that functioned as Evelina's "flower room."*

Introduction

chrysanthemums and verbena."

Whether cut for a vase, potted in a conservatory, or massed in the garden, dahlias were her favorite flower. She seems to have been swept up in the dahlia craze that reigned in Europe in the first decades of the nineteenth century. By 1829 the dahlia was proclaimed "the most fashionable flower in England." In 1837 Evelina reported from France that Antoine's sister Adele had "the most beautiful dahlias in profusion" in her garden outside Paris. At Winterthur in the 1840s and 1850s, Evelina planted her own profusion, "dahlias around the house, dahlias around shrubbery in the kitchen yard and . . . on the hillside near the garden."

A full-time gardener helped Evelina maintain her flowers: the French-speaking Jacques of the 1840s was replaced about 1850 by Alexander, a Scot. The Bidermanns were again in search of a gardener in 1859, as indicated by an advertisement in *Gardener's Monthly* that October.

I have a kitchen garden and a small greenhouse or conservatory to be attended to. I keep only two men viz. the gardener and one to attend to my carriage horses. The latter gives occasional help, principally to attend to the flower plots near the house and to moving the plants in and out of the greenhouse. I give my present gardener $23. a month and a house.

The gardener hired in 1859 did not have a long residence at Winterthur. For, after a short illness, Evelina died in December 1863, age sixty-seven. Antoine, increasingly frail, returned to France to be with their only son, James Irénée. In the two years before his death in 1865, Antoine sent numerous letters to Delaware, giving advice about the maintenance of the Winterthur farm and begging for news on the state of the garden and the tropical plants in the greenhouse. "We will not let any of the flowers freeze," Sophie assured him. "We will all take some and nurse them carefully . . . for we love dearly those flowers from Winterthur."

The Gilded Age at Winterthur: The Colonel and Pauline

AFTER THE DEATH OF THE BIDERMANNS, Winterthur was bought from their son, James Irénée, by Henry du Pont, Evelina's younger brother. Henry acquired the estate for his eldest son, Henry Algernon, whom the Bidermanns had called their favorite nephew. Henry Algernon had practically grown up on his aunt and uncle's estate. As a child, he had even planted a garden there. Evelina reminded him of this in a letter when he was away fighting in the Civil War and in need of cheering up: "In your old garden still peep forth a few flowers of your planting at four years old. There is still a bunch of dark blue Hepatica which remind me of your eyes as they were then."

Pauline Foster du Pont in her wedding dress, 1874.

A history buff with a talent for engineering and an interest in botany, Henry Algernon enjoyed a successful career in the army, where he achieved the rank of Colonel and won the Congressional Medal of Honor for his part in the Battle of Cedar Creek. The Colonel, as he was known the rest of his life, was well suited for the responsibilities of maintaining a large country estate. He and his wife, Mary Pauline Foster du Pont, took up residence at Winterthur in 1876; the young Pauline was only too delighted to care for the expansive flower garden.

Born into "old New York" society, a childhood friend of Edith Wharton and an intimate of the Astors, Pauline's New York background is an essential part of the flower arranging history of Winterthur. The year she married, 1874, the *British Journal of Horticulture* was abuzz with news about "the profuseness with which flowers are used in New York." Pauline's wedding presents reflected the new mode. She received a treasure trove of silver, crystal and porcelain vases, tazzas, flower dishes, and jardinieres. A pair of silver bud vases from Tiffany's, engraved with her initials, are still in the Winterthur collection. The quantity of flowers used at Pauline's wedding reception left the du Pont family slightly taken aback:

The house was beautifully decorated with flowers. The mantelpieces were covered with flowers laid close together so as to hide the marble shelf. Pauline's friends . . . sent her bouquets and baskets of flowers until the top of the piano was covered . . . it was impossible to enjoy them all at once.

The Colonel and Pauline's yearlong honeymoon carried them from Niagara Falls to England, France, and Italy. In England they stayed at Bromborough Hall, a seventeenth-century country house known for its lavish gardens. "There is a lively little conservatory opening onto the library where I am writing filled with beautiful flowers," Pauline explained to her sister Anna. "I keep my eyes wide open and am getting ideas constantly." As it had been with the Bidermanns, one of the first concerns of Pauline and the Colonel was the Winterthur conservatory. The Colonel's father suggested that "the old forcing house in the garden be put in order so that Pauline may have some flowers this winter."

Although both Pauline and the Colonel were inclined toward moderation, the spirit of the times and their own financial circumstances dictated a certain grandiosity. In the last quarter of the nineteenth century, the Gilded Age, "more" was considered almost always better: in the house, at

Engraved Tiffany bud vases given to Pauline Foster du Pont as a wedding gift, 1874.

Introduction

the table, in the garden. Under the Colonel's management, the Winterthur estate expanded greatly: more acreage, more agriculture, a larger garden, more greenhouses, more workers. Pauline's letters indicate that lilies of the valley grew undisturbed along the banks of Clenny Run, just as they had in Evelina's day. Crocus and violets continued their spring blooms north of the house. And Pauline adopted and increased Evelina's circle of ten ever-blooming roses.

By the 1890s, August Dauphin was established as head house butler. One of his primary duties was "receiving, unpacking, and distributing" the flowers. As noted in literature of the day, "Flowers are so profusely distributed in the households of the rich, that their arrangement absorbs a great deal of time."

Within the Wilmington community, Pauline's flower style was exceptional. Lilies seem to have been her favorite. The ones she grew were so fragrant one recipient claimed they were identifiable by the smell alone. "My dear Mrs. du Pont, the lilies are scenting the house and Harry's arrived by the same mail . . . I know more than ever they are sweeter than anyone else's."

The lily and the sunflower were emblematic of the late nineteenth-century reform movement of

The Winterthur house in 1887 with Pauline's cold frame "forcing shed" in the foreground.

decoration. Pauline's collection of porcelain, antique velvets, and "quaint" furniture indicates that she shared in those tastes. In January 1902, before the Colonel and Pauline undertook a house renovation, a set of photographs was made. The images show rooms decorated in mainstream "artistic" taste. The flowers were also up-to-date. In reaction to the overblown arrangements of the 1870s and 1880s, a relatively spare, aesthetic style reigned in the fashionable world at the beginning of the twentieth century. In the Winterthur parlor of 1902, an enormous, costly, but simple orchid dominates the room.

Pauline Foster du Pont died in September 1902. She became forever associated with the rose and lily of the valley when her son placed two

blossoms in his Bible and wrote:

> *This lily of the Valley is the last flower that Mama smelled & really enjoyed. Friday morning September 19*

> *This rose fell off Mamma's coffin in the vestibule of the church after the service.*

An enormous orchid dominates the Winterthur parlor in 1902.

Introduction

The Edwardian Splendor of Henry Francis

IN 1962, DURING THE ONLY FORMAL INTERVIEW of his life, Henry Francis du Pont was asked about his mother. His answer was simple: "She loved flowers—I know that. That's the reason I got interested in them, too." He further explained,

> *I have always loved flowers and had a garden as a child . . . if you have grown up with flowers and really seen them, you can't help to have unconsciously absorbed an appreciation of proportion, color, detail, and material.*

H. F. du Pont's life could serve as a model for the popular Victorian education theory to which his mother obviously subscribed. Nineteenth-century household advice books recommended gardening as a method of instruction for children. Tending plants, it was thought, would encourage an aesthetic and spiritual appreciation of nature. "Benevolent and social feelings could also be cultivated, by influencing children to share their fruits and flowers with friends and neighbors, as well as to distribute roots and seeds to those who have not the means of procuring them." Henry Francis, or Harry, as he was known to his friends, spent his life putting those ideas into practice.

The letters Pauline wrote to her son after he had left for boarding school showed a continuation of those lessons. She kept him informed about the events at Winterthur: the seasonal farm news, the latest changes in the garden, and the current state

of the surrounding woodland. Sometimes the letters included pressed flowers. As Harry grew older and his attention to taste and decoration became apparent, Pauline began to include descriptions of the flowers at formal dinner parties she attended:

> *My dear Harry,*
> *We had a very nice time at Cousin Giraud's last night. . . In the center of the table there was a superb basket of white roses and mignonette. The mignonette were about five times the ordinary size.*

Floral Christmas card collected by H. F. du Pont, 1895.

> *with loads of love and kisses from Papa, always loads of love, Mama.*

Henry Francis was devastated when his mother died. After completing his studies at Harvard in 1903, he returned to Winterthur and assumed her projects. The years between her death in 1902 and the death of his father in 1926 served as a training period, preparing Harry for the responsibilities of overseeing the vast estate. He mastered agriculture and farm management skills as well as domestic arts: interior decorating, gardening, and flower arranging. Rigorously improving the estate and adopting professional standards, he sought out experts in every field.

H. F. du Pont made flowers an integral part of

Introduction

H. F. du Pont with a cousin in the garden at Winterthur, 1900.

Winterthur's room design. His secretary of nearly fifty years claimed that her boss was "never without flowers." No effort was spared to keep blooms fresh and arrangements in the latest fashion. H. F. wrote regularly to expert seedsmen such as Harry Dreer, met with Gertrude Jekyll, and consulted with the best silversmiths on designs for vases. "Please send four of the largest size vases with crystal handles similar to the ones I bought from you two years ago and have the framework silver-plated," began one rather extravagant order to Phillips Ltd. in London.

Between 1903 and 1910, the Colonel and his son oversaw the construction of an entire village of greenhouses, containing separate cement structures for soil, potting, and pot washing. Specialized houses for ferns, roses, figs, and chrysanthemums were erected. Enormous storage pits dotted the perimeter of the greenhouse area. They held the hundreds of potted plants that were used in rotation in the conservatory, entrance hall, and outdoor terraces. When in full operation, the greenhouses were manned with a staff of six. Six more worked in the cutting gardens.

In 1908 du Pont advertised for a new assistant gardener who would help

in the care of the greenhouse, hothouses, and work outside . . . and would have to be

Autochrome showing a profusion of peonies and flowering vines surrounding a garden pavilion at Winterthur, 1913.

familiar with the care of roses, carnations, chrysanthemums, palm, ferns, poinsettias, azaleas, cinerarias, etc. The wages would be, for a single man, $35 per month and board; for a married man, $40 a month, house rent-free.

Even with all the greenhouses and cutting gardens, Henry Francis continued the family tradition of seeking out Brandywine Valley wildflowers. In 1911 he made a request of his coachman, Clarence Norris,

When you see this letter please go at once for me and see if you cannot pick me a large

bunch of dry mild weed stalks. I have had some for the last two years in vases in my sitting room. . . Even if the bulbs are quite closed, do not hesitate to pick them as they really are better when they open in the house.

H. F.'s flowers were arranged much as his great-aunt Evelina's were in the 1840s and 1850s. Cut in the garden, the flowers were tied with string and brought into the house and placed in water-filled containers. The string was then cut, and the

Winterthur garden staff, 1920.

Introduction

flowers were left as they fell. Unlike Evelina, however, Henry Francis did not arrange the flowers himself; he supervised the process.

Throughout his life, du Pont favored lush, homogeneous flower arrangements with a single type of flower. An autochrome of the Winterthur Drawing Room from May 13, 1913, allows us to see what H. F. was doing with flowers in the early days. In his 1962 interview, he advocated moderation, "There's a limit to the number of flowers that you can have in one place." The 1913 photograph suggests that this knowledge may have come through bitter experience. It is hard to imagine more flowers occupying the room. Dark red tulips are tightly massed between the boughs of pink azaleas and purple lilacs. The glass in the

door reflects a haze of flowers to the left, and, through the door, the hall is an equal marvel—crammed with palms, daisy chrysanthemums, and purple azaleas.

No special occasion seems to have marked that date. The only "event" was the photo session itself. The autochrome process was new and expensive, and no doubt the Winterthur rooms were specially prepared and rearranged. Even so, the flowers seem to correspond in quantity and quality to those seen by guests at the time.

J. P. Morgan's wife, Jessie, no stranger to Edwardian excess, visited Winterthur in 1914 and wrote the following note: "We shall long remember the feast of flowers! . . . The most beautiful combinations of colours, in both house &

gardens." In 1961 H. F. received a letter from a guest who remembered the house as it had been in the first decade of the twentieth century. "I always see your father, the exact French *gentilhomme*, in the most beautiful library I ever saw, with wisteria and lilacs all over the place, and your own marvelous flower arrangements in house and garden."

After the Colonel died, flowers took on even greater importance. More greenhouses were built; a total of twenty-two were in place by 1951. The cutting garden was expanded until it stretched over four acres, and a refrigerated cold-storage shed was erected in the field to keep the flowers as fresh as possible. A flower-arranging room, with another walk-in refrigerated storage area, was added to the main house in 1929.

For almost twenty-nine years, Stella Price, hired as a parlor maid in 1924, arranged the flowers for the main reception areas of the house. H. F. du Pont's morning routine included visiting the flower room, checking on the flowers the gardeners had placed in the cooler, and then inspecting the final display. When making her creations, Stella insisted on absolute silence, which was enforced by regular reminder memos to the Winterthur staff from du Pont. Each of the five

Autochrome of the Winterthur Drawing Room in 1913.

Introduction

or six reception rooms under her care could require as many as twenty-five bouquets. Every arrangement was made for a specific room and preordained place. Stella and her assistant, John Smith, carefully positioned and fluffed each one.

Another aspect of the morning routine were the meetings between H. F. and the head of the greenhouse to discuss the flower arrangements for the conservatory. Records of successful arrangements were kept by a secretary, and the conservatory file includes month-by-month lists of installations. An interesting aspect of the notes is the use of theatrical terms, as on October 24, 1945: "Cleaned out all gentista, bouvardias, buddleias, ginger plants to make way for our first show of the season." Again on December 4, du Pont noted, "This is only a temporary

arrangement as our main Xmas show will come a little later."

An equally important part of the daily routine was the morning meeting with the butler to discuss flowers for the table. Available blooms from the garden were matched with the vast collection of linen and porcelain for the daily lunch and dinner table. Again, a detailed notebook was kept of the coordinating arrangements. On the grandest occasions, such as the du Pont daughters' weddings, special flowers were grown. One greenhouse was devoted to a rose of a particular pink that H. F. liked with one set of china.

A section of the cutting garden in the 1930s.

A profusion of flowers fills the Winterthur conservatory in the 1930s.

Each of H. F. du Pont's table settings was a stage set that was not to be viewed until the meal was served. One dinner guest remembers being reprimanded for trying to get a glimpse beforehand. "No," she was told quite seriously, "you will have to wait until the time arrives."

The result of the fastidious effort on the part of Henry Francis, the gardeners, the butler, footmen, flower arrangers, and secretaries was extraordinary. The entire house was filled with floral spectacles. As one weekend guest noted:

I stopped dead in my tracks and must have looked like a fool with my mouth open—and as I stood breathless at this beauty I looked around at the room and Mrs. du Pont burst out laughing! I just gasped! It was the Chinese room—with the unbelievable Chinese scenic paper on the walls—and everywhere in every flat space big enough to hold a vase of flowers: Huge crystal bowls of pure white chrysanthemums; bowls of the most delicate, pink chrysanthemums; tiny vases with a single hibiscus—three or four of these on a single table. I was wordless—indeed breathless.

This table setting highlights H. F. du Pont's arrangement of flowers and china, 1962.

Introduction

A 1935 stereopticon view of the Chinese Parlor filled with bouquets.

Even after 1951, when the house was opened as a museum, Winterthur rooms bloomed with the color and fresh scent of flowers. "I always want this Museum to look as if someone is living in it, with flowers in the room. . . . There must be someone employed who has taste and will use the right colors in the rooms as is done now," H. F. du Pont wrote to his executors. When Stella Price retired from Winterthur in 1953, her position was filled by Jody Shoemaker, who first became involved with Winterthur through her volunteer work with the Junior League. Shoemaker changed the style of flower arrangements in the museum, creating mixed bouquets in a more formal eighteenth-century fashion. Nevertheless, du Pont approved of the new style for the museum— "I don't know what you are doing young lady, but I like it."

In H. F. du Pont's final portrait, painted four years before his death in 1969, he is depicted in the conservatory of his new home on the estate, The Cottage, where the family moved after the museum opened to the public. He is standing beside a bank of pink cymbidium orchids and bamboo. More flowers, including orchids and clivias, can be glimpsed through the glass wall. Deep in the background, the drawing room is frothy with pink lilies cascading from large vases. Flowers surround and stretch out behind. The conservatory, always important to life at Winterthur, is an appropriate setting for the painting.

An elegant arrangement by Jody Shoemaker.

One of the last acts of du Pont's life was to preserve what may have been Evelina du Pont Bidermann's favorite greenhouse azalea. "It was a monster, potted in a great big tub," remembers gardener Albert Feliciani, and its ultimate fate was of great concern to du Pont. "The big white azalea which has been in the family three generations is superb in the conservatory in April, but I have decided to plant it in the corner of the lawn as you go out the golf door." And there a white azalea blooms today, a true reminder of the importance that flowers have held for generations of du Ponts.

Portrait of H. F. du Pont in the conservatory of The Cottage, 1965.

Introduction

Period Rooms

Henry Francis du Pont's extraordinary collection of decorative arts is displayed in the 175 period rooms at Winterthur. As can be seen in the following chapters, du Pont purchased historically accurate architecture and interiors to provide appropriate settings for his acquisitions. He further enhanced the settings with splendid bouquets in complementary vases, punch bowls, and tureens.

In the Oyster Bay Room we see yellow yarrow, orange lilies, and salpiglossis arranged in a pewter container. Seventeenth-century colonists placed rugs (such as the Turkish one seen here) on the top of tables for display purposes.

Although little is known of how flowers were arranged in the 1600s, we do have documentation that the Dutch displayed tulips, roses, violets, marigolds, and gilly flowers in simple containers. Native flowers such as black-eyed Susans, asters, goldenrod, and laurel would also have been abundant in the colonies.

Period Rooms

A good source of information about plant material exchanged between the colonies and England is the correspondence of Philadelphia native John Bartram and London horticulturist Peter Collinson. In 1728 Bartram planted the first botanical garden near Philadelphia. He sent more than 150 species of native trees, shrubs, and wildflowers to England. Collinson returned the favor with crocus, narcissus, lilies, gladiolus, tuberoses, roses, asters, pinks, and carnations, of which Bartram wrote in 1761, "I have now a glorious appearance of carnations from thy seed—the brightest colors that ever eyes beheld."

In the William and Mary Parlor, the marbleized and grained paneling of a circa 1725 house serves as a backdrop for the arrangement of bronze chrysanthemums, sedum, and red foxtail grasses. The style of furniture and furnishings show a new sophistication and interest in color, pattern, and texture.

The Queen Anne style, in Readbourne Stair Hall, is known for its simplicity and elegance, with a balance of curves. English painter William Hogarth identified the cyma curve as the "line of beauty." Flower arrangers use the S-shape as a design form.

This arrangement of dogwood foliage, red roses, daisies, and pampas grass blends with the red damask window hangings and slip seats on the chairs. Color is the "key" element that guides the choice of flowers. The setting is further enhanced by the John Singleton Copley painting of the Gore children.

Period Rooms

This small arrangement in the Marlboro Room shows the seed heads of the blackberry lily, which appears in the fall. They look like a juicy blackberry although they are hard and dry. Other plant materials are chrysanthemums and pachysandra, a ground cover from the garden that works well as greenery.

In the 1700s, boughpots were filled with large branches of fruit blossoms and masses of wildflowers during the summer to hide soot in the fireplace. In the Marlboro Room we see native Queen Anne's lace and black-eyed Susans. Above the fireplace is a needlepoint of a "fishing lady" picture made in 1748 by Sarah Warren in Barnstable, Massachusetts.

Period Rooms

Port Royal Parlor, with Chippendale-style furniture, is arranged with perfect order. The matching pair of large, mass bouquets are made to scale and are ideally suited for the balanced symmetry of furniture and architecture. When creating such arrangements, it is necessary to continuously rotate the bowl on a lazy Susan to achieve the proper effect. Large flowers such as the lilies should be placed at the base, some tucked in, others coming over the side of the bowl. The spikes of delphinium provide height, balance, and lightness.

Architecture from a 1783 house in Kutztown, Pennsylvania, creates the perfect setting for a collection of Pennsylvania German furniture, with chests displaying motifs of tulips, hearts, and unicorns. On the walls are Fraktur—colorfully decorated documents (birth, baptismal, and marriage certificates) produced by schoolteachers or clergymen. Nothing formal would be appropriate here. Suitable choices are the orange flower of the blackberry lily, black-eyed Susans, dahlias, and gloriosa daisies. The earthenware jar is covered with sgraffito decoration of stylized flowers. Pennsylvania Germans were garden enthusiasts and would have grown a variety of flowers.

Period Rooms

The delicate and light federal furniture
with pale upholstery colors encourages
the use of light, delicate, soft colors of
flowers. Those in the arrangement are
cushion flower, Queen Anne's lace, and
lisianthus. The pink, white, and violet-
blue lisianthus, some with colored ruffled
edges, are magnificent and long-lasting.
The unopened blossoms resemble
rosebuds; opened flowers are like frilly
tulips; fully opened, they look like
poppies. The arrangement mixes well with
the stripes, flowers, and vines in the
upholstery.

The early 19th-century architecture in the Baltimore Drawing
Room features a plaster mantelpiece decorated with classical
motifs: swags, urns, and the eagle—symbol for the New
Republic. Fragrant summer roses reflect lushness at its best.
The buds form the top; large roses open full and fill in the
base. The silverplate urn serves as an appropriate classical
form; the neutral silver allows the colors of the roses to mix
easily.

Period Rooms

Wallpaper

"My father's love of color led to his fondness for wallpaper," noted Ruth du Pont Lord. At Winterthur, numerous hallways and fifteen full rooms display lush, handpainted wallpaper in a variety of designs and colors. "In this house where vistas of the landscape are omnipresent, du Pont felt compelled to add landscapes in the hallways—generally European and oriental wallpapers—reinforcing the association of the interiors with nature."

Bold calla lilies dictate the overall design of this arrangement in the Philadelphia Bedroom. Lilies are placed sideways at a slant for better effect, with the lily at the base facing front and serving as the focal point. The fragrant blossoms of pink viburnum with matching tulips achieve balance and unity. The handpainted decoration of birds and flowers on the Chinese porcelain cachepot and on the late 18th-century Chinese wallpaper further enhance the setting.

Wallpaper

In 1928 H. F. du Pont purchased the 18th-century handpainted Chinese wallpaper for the Port Royal Entrance Hall from the London firm of Cowtan and Tout.

Massing fragrant, lush peonies, the "king of flowers," using tight buds and full blooms, forms a solid design that mirrors the blooms on the 18th-century handpainted Chinese wallpaper in the Port Royal Entrance Hall.

The graceful, natural curve of purple lupine gives the arrangement the height needed to balance the large, showy peony. Other flowers fill in to complete the composition, which works well with the late 18th-century handpainted Chinese wallpaper in the Chinese Parlor.

Wallpaper

The five-finger posy holder was first created in the 17th century for Queen Mary, a lover of flowers.

The classical swags and urns of flowers in the French blockprint wallpaper influence the design of the arrangement in the five-finger posy holder. Tall arborvitae, with wispy, delicate tips, is placed in the five openings, creating the fan-shape design. Paperwhites and pale pink stock add fullness. Peachy tulips tucked in the bottom give balance and accent. The Etruscan-pattern wallpaper, from the French firm of Réveillon, was originally installed in the home of Oliver Phelps, Sheffield, Connecticut, in the 1790s.

In the Imlay Room, the combination of flowers in one color with varying sizes and shapes produces pleasing textures. The variety includes rose-pink spikes of false dragonhead, asters, tulips, strawflowers, lisianthus, and large cactus-type dahlias. The arrangement fully complements the color scheme of the wallpaper, which was purchased by John Imlay in 1794 for his home in Allentown, New Jersey.

Wallpaper

Mirrors

Hanging mirrors, looking glasses, pier glasses, and girandole mirrors, some 200 in all, adorn the many period rooms at Winterthur. When fellow members of the Walpole Society first saw H. F. du Pont's Winterthur in 1932, their enthusiasm was profuse. "Imagine a house that records the decorative history of our country, and in supreme terms! Interested in looking glasses? . . . Fine specimens of every kind."

The "neutral" color of the black urn and dark marble surface allows the colors of the massive arrangement—pink stock, blue iris, and drooping pink tulips mixed lightly with branches of azalea—to become dominant in the space. The early 19th-century gilt looking glass with architectural cornice comes from New England.

Mirrors

Spring-blooming quince stands high and wide in the tall cachepot; the pink tulips provide depth and accent, achieving an overall balance. The ethereal effect of the arrangement mimics that of the delicate foliage motif popular in the federal period, seen here on the looking glass.

This striking arrangement with an abundance of colorful flowers contains pink shades of azalea and viburnum mixed with deep pink and purple lupine, blue delphinium, and pale yellow and orange poppies. The form and shape of the arrangement is balanced, but overall it states a "do as you please" feeling.

Mirrors

The Port Royal Entrance Hall mirror, with walnut veneer frame and gilt carving, was once in the Bromfield-Phillips House in Beacon Street, Boston, where Abigail Phillips and Josiah Quincy were married in 1769.

A lush, mass arrangement of peonies with garden flowers fills the Chinese export porcelain bowl in the Port Royal Entrance Hall. The arrangement is appropriate to the space, noting the high ceiling, elaborate mirror, and handpainted Chinese wallpaper featuring peonies. It is a successful integration of form, color, texture, and shape.

Fragrant and great in scale and proportion, the arrangement contains harmonious colors of red tulips, reddish azalea, white lilac, and stock to create a balanced, unified composition. It reflects the proportion and balance of the gilt looking glass from New York and the lighting devices on the table.

Mirrors

Branches

The eighteenth-century handpainted wallpaper in the Chinese Parlor creates the perfect setting for the Eastern, elegant line created with natural branches. H. F. du Pont was particularly fond of arrangements of one variety and color and was known to have asked his coachman to search the surrounding landscape for a "large bunch of dry milk week stalks" for his sitting room.

Towering heights of cherry blossoms are informally arranged in a container suitable for the branches and their scale of space. Tight buds will open easily and provide wonderful spring blossoms. The arrangement and vase fully complement the room furnishings, creating a quiet, subdued ensemble.

Branches

The harmonious arrangement of plume poppy in the Chinese export porcelain vase reflects the Chinese temperament in flower arranging: relaxed feeling, simplicity of plant material, and elegant container.

Branches

Sprawling bright-yellow forsythia branches bring cheer during the winter months. To force forsythia, cut branches and bring indoors. Place stems in water and allow several weeks for the forsythia to bloom. Worth the wait!

A swirl of dried pampas grass plumes, with leaves that curl when drying, are freely arranged and easily done.

Branches

Windows

H. F. du Pont continually sought to bring the "outdoors" inside. He changed the period room textile furnishings seasonally to coordinate with the views and colors seen from the windows and favored floral arrangements that highlighted the changing variety in the garden. Du Pont's acute color perception is reflected in the forty-some different shades of green on the paneling and walls throughout the museum.

A successful composition of color, texture, and unity can be attained with dried puffs and curled leaves of pampas grass, pointed orangy snapdragon, bronze cushion chrysanthemums, and berries of gold bittersweet. The warm, autumn tones seen through the window are repeated in this seasonally appropriate arrangement.

Windows

The selection of the colorful tobacco-leaf pattern cachepot allows complementary flowers to form a total picture. Full blooms of pink and white peonies are mixed with towering, stately, spotted bell-shaped foxglove and extravagant blue delphinium. Green shades of hydrangea and nicotania blend in without interfering. Feathery plumes of goat's beard, added last in the arrangement, add lightness and height.

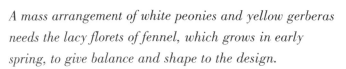

A mass arrangement of white peonies and yellow gerberas needs the lacy florets of fennel, which grows in early spring, to give balance and shape to the design.

Windows

Fall colors seen in full plumes of pampas grass and a mixture of daisylike chrysanthemums highlight the house-garden relationship at Winterthur, with the fall foliage in the background through the window. The deep-colored chrysanthemums at the base pull the eye to the center of the arrangement.

When Peter Kalm, a Swedish naturalist and traveler, visited the colonies in the mid 18th century, he wrote in his *Travels into North America,* "The Ladies are much inclined to have fine Flowers all summer long, about, or upon the Chimneys, upon a Table or before a Window, either because of their Beauty or their sweet scent ."

The outline of this wonderful arrangement is formed by the placement of small flower heads of black-eyed Susans at the top, fanning out. Larger flowers at the bottom give depth and focal point. The spring orange flower of blackberry lily and green goldenrod, picked early before turning gold, complete the overall design. The dark brown dock from the fields complements well.

Windows

How-To

PREPARATION OF PLANT MATERIAL

Proper conditioning of plant material is essential for an arrangement. Use only fresh; flowers that are limp, soft, or too full-blown will not last.

≫ Plant material should be cut **early morning** or **late afternoon**, never in the heat of the day. Cut stem ends at an angle. Split stem ends of branches several times vertically, two to three inches, for greater water absorption. Use clean, **sharp pruners**. Avoid scissors, as they could pinch the stems.

≫ As soon as possible after cutting, place plant material in **fresh water** with a preservative. Remove any thorns. Powdery stamens should be pulled off to prevent staining of the petals.

≫ **Strip foliage** that is below the water line. Remove leaves that are wilted, damaged, or have holes. Wrap leggy stems, such as tulips, with paper to secure them while being conditioned.

≫ **Buckets** for holding cut plant material should be bacteria free. Use a variety of sizes—small for short stems, tall for branches or leggy material.

≫ Evergreen foliage may be dust-laden or dirty; **swish** in water to clean and freshen.

≫ Allow plant material to soak for several hours or, preferably, overnight in a **cool** place.

PRINCIPLES OF DESIGN

Flower arranging is a creative art. As in every art form, there are rules to guide us.

To achieve a good artistic composition, guidelines should be followed. There are four basic design elements: **form**, **texture**, **space**, and **color**. The six principles of design are **balance**, **scale**, **proportion**, **rhythm**, **dominance**, and **contrast**.

⁂ Consider first the **design** of the composition as a whole. Select the **container** to accommodate the site. The **setting** will determine the size of the arrangement. Proper scale among flowers, foliage, site, and container is essential.

⁂ The **container** is integral to the design. Try to include the container colors in the overall color scheme if plant material permits. White, silver, gray, and black containers are considered neutral. Black containers are extremely useful and combine well with vibrant colors and textures. Green containers often clash with leaves and stems.

⁂ **Form** and **color** are closely related. The shapes and sizes of the flowers, branches, and foliage are important, but color should be the first consideration; it makes the first impression.

⁂ Use **color** to emphasize **design**. Color will enhance and allow the arrangement to flow. Warm hues—red, orange, and yellow—convey a feeling of goodwill and cheer. Cool hues—violet, blue, and green—promote a feeling of peace and tranquility. Using many of the same tints, tones, and shades of chosen hues will produce a colorful **harmony**.

⁂ Perfection will not be achieved if the arrangement lacks **color balance**, which determines depth, lightness, and weight. A large, deep-colored flower placed low in the arrangement will give depth and weight; a bud or light-colored flower in a high position will add lightness and height.

≫ Size is also important in **balance**. The placement of graduated forms and shapes creates balance and unity, both vertically and horizontally: delicate or fine at the top and edge of the design, then medium, and then dense and heavy at the base. It is important to bring the eye to the **focal point**, where the design is most dominant—the center or the low part of the arrangement. Select focal flowers or foliage based on size, bold forms, and intense color.

≫ **Repetition** of the same color, shape, or texture can establish a **rhythm** that flows through the main lines of the arrangement. A successful design with good rhythmic movement has no visual distraction. Curved branches and stems suggest movement; straight ones are static. Repeat and contrast using a variety of forms, texture, and color. But be careful; too much repetition can make a design boring.

≫ Select **foliage** wisely. Strong, bold foliage can be used to form the outline of the arrangement. Longer, supple foliage adds width and a sense of movement. Foliage can be used as a filler to provide texture and color contrast.

≫ Experiment with **texture**. Foliage texture ranges from waxy and glossy to fine and prickly. The texture of leaves of the same size can visually appear different. Strong, tough leaves look heavier than smooth ones of the same size. Combine foliage and flowers and see how they relate. It is best not to use strong, textured leaves with delicate flowers. Heavy-textured leaves placed at the base "anchor" and give weight to the design. Fine-textured or feathery ones placed at the top and elsewhere provide contrast and lightness.

CREATING THE ARRANGEMENT

Now that we have discussed the basic principles, we can begin.

≫ A general rule is that the height of the design should be 1 ^{1}/2 times the height of the container.

≫ Create an outline or background with branchlike plant material.

≫ Strip unnecessary or awkward parts.

≫ Groom or remove wilted, damaged leaves.

≫ Cut branches at an angle.

≫ Then select plant material for fill and focal flowers and foliage for the center of interest.

≫ Arrange tall forms or large masses first. All plant material, branches, flowers, and foliage should be placed in at a slant to achieve proper balance and scale.

≫ Flowers of different heights create depth. Follow the natural line of the flowers; they should not all be facing the same direction.

≫ Don't crowd the plant material.

≫ Use foliage where needed to fill in, to set off the flowers, and to soften the line between the container and the flowers. Always strip leaves off lower part of stem, cut stem at an angle, then insert.

≫ Know when to stop!

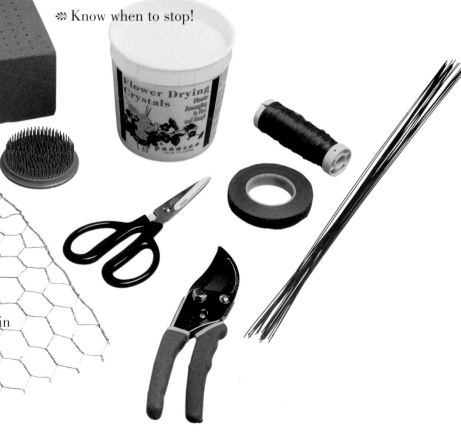

CLASSIC ELEGANCE   **Plant material: delphinium, calla lilies, spirea, roses, ruscus**

≫ Create a triangular line with various lengths of ruscus foliage and spires of delphinium.

≫ Scale is the most important feature. Height is achieved by the delphinium; width is established by the calla lilies and spirea.

≫ The height of the vase allows the flowers and foliage to extend out and calls for longer, more elegant stems and foliage. The longer stems should be placed high and toward the back.

≫ The classic, trumpet-shaped calla lilies combine well with the full, round shapes of the roses. Carefully place throughout for balance.

≫ Decide where flowers should be before cutting.

≫ The bright yellow adds a wonderful brilliance to the arrangement and the silver vase.

≫ Add the white spirea. The natural, curving lines will enhance the shape of the design and texture of the flowers and create rhythmic movement. White flowers always lighten and provide accent to colored flowers.

≫ Have flowers and foliage come down to conceal the top of the vase and the stems.

How-To

SPRING LUSHNESS

Plant material: eucalyptus, peonies

≫ Fill the bowl with florist foam (oasis) that has been soaked in water with preservative. Place chicken wire over the oasis to provide extra support for the heavy stems.

≫ Carefully select branches of eucalyptus for the outline. Vary the length of stems, some in, some out, some angled. This will give the dimensions for the design and create voids in which to place the peonies.

≫ Add buds and small flower heads at the top to form the highest point. These give height, balance, and lightness.

≫ As you place other peonies, turn some sideways. Allow others to bend gently to spill out over the design and the bowl.

≫ Do not cut stems until you are sure of the length needed. Hold the flower in place against the arrangement, then cut.

≫ Study your arrangement frequently from all angles. The placement of the white peonies with the deep scarlet ones unifies the overall design.

≫ Place several large, deep scarlet peonies through the center of the design to provide the focal point.

≫ Take additional peony foliage to soften and feather out the base of the arrangement.

How-To

GRACEFUL GRANDEUR

Plant material: viburnum, lilacs, azaleas, snapdragon, tulips, anemones, iris, sweet peas, hyacinths, orchids

⋙ Create an outline with viburnum branches.

⋙ Strip all leaves from the lilacs and place among the viburnum.

⋙ Add lavender azaleas. Then begin to fill with a mixture of colors, shapes, and textures.

⋙ Place the deep pinks of the snapdragon, tulips, and anemones throughout, some close in and others at the base. This will provide the proper depth, weight, and balance.

⋙ Sparingly place the deep purple anemones and iris in the lower part of the arrangement.

⋙ Add colorful sweet peas and blue hyacinths to give an element of delicacy.

⋙ White calla lilies will break up the denseness of the other colors.

⋙ The final touch of white dendodrium orchids lightens and widens the overall design. As you can see, the green viburnum continues to break out from the colorful flowers.

⋙ The final snapdragon drooping from the arrangement gracefully leads the eye down from the mass arrangement.

How-To

HOLIDAY ARRANGEMENT   **Plant material: pine, poinsettia**

≫ The brass monteith is large, so the arrangement needs volume. The pine should fill most of the container to allow a good structure. To achieve a feeling of lightness, go high in the center and extend out over the sides.

≫ Select the cut poinsettias carefully before arranging. Avoid weak or straggly stems. Remove most of the leaves. Wipe the milky sap from the stems. Place the smaller flowers at the top. Gradually add the larger ones at the base to provide a focal point.

≫ Allow the green tips of pine to be intermixed and stand away from the flowers, providing better balance and unity.

Note: It is best to arrange cut stems of poinsettias using a pinholder (not oasis) in a container with ample water.

TULIPS   **Plant material: quince and tulips**

≫ Make the arrangement in a pinholder since tulips are difficult to place in oasis.

≫ Arrange quince branches first to provide structure and an overall design outline.

≫ Place tulips at a slant from top to bottom while working side to side. Keep filling in until there are few openings.

≫ The top tulips should take on a triangular shape to give proper balance. Allow the lower ones to droop freely. Let the green stems show.

≫ Words of caution when using tulips: they can grow up to three inches in water, becoming unruly. They are affected by heat and strong light. Blooms open full.

The tulip was one of the most sought-after flowers. It was introduced into Holland from Persia (Iran). The Dutch tulip craze of 1634–37 is well recorded in history.

How-To

CACHEPOT

Plant material: bells of Ireland, snapdragon, delphinium, tulips, gerbera, ranunculus, nerine lily, pale pink lily, hyacinths, veronica, and ixia

>» To keep the arrangement from becoming too packed, strip most of the leaves from the stems.

>» Curved stems of bells of Ireland serve as foliage and create the overall outline. Start forming the vertical lines with the orange snapdragon and blue delphinium, placing them at a slant.

>» The snapdragon, delphinium, and bells of Ireland will create open spaces for the fuller flowers.

>» Using at least three or five stems of each, begin to add tulips, pink gerberas, varying shades of deep pink ranunculus, bright pink nerine lily, pale pink lily with buds (allow to stand out a bit), blue hyacinths, and blue veronica at top.

>» Intersperse pale pink ixia at the top and throughout the arrangement to give additional height and lightness.

>» Colors are carried throughout the arrangement. The outline is solid with no empty spaces.

MASS SUMMER ARRANGEMENT

Plant material: white hydrangea, cleome, roses, hosta blooms, Queen Anne's lace, and arborvitae

≫ Place white hydrangea going up about 3/4 of the arrangement. *Note: hydrangea should be well conditioned and all leaves stripped so water can get to the blossoms.*

≫ Privet should then be placed to provide support and structure to the arrangement.

≫ Repeat the whiteness with the white cleome, or spider plant, to create harmony.

≫ Add pink roses to further enhance.

≫ Place long stems of hosta blooms and Queen Anne's lace to give height and airiness.

≫ Use the evergreen arborvitae at the base.

How-To

HARMONIOUS BLEND

Plant material: mock orange and peonies

≫ Carefully select branches of mock orange and place throughout to form the outline.

≫ Leave open spaces for the large white peonies.

≫ Place peonies, some slightly turned sideways, some tucked in, others coming forward.

≫ Fill in with additional mock orange to complete and lighten the mass.

≫ The small, white blossoms of the mock orange contrast well with the large white peonies.

Note: Consider the height of the vase and boundaries of the niche before starting to arrange.

WARM HUES

Plant material: gladioli, sunflowers, dahlias, and goldenrod

≫ Five stems of gladioli, using several colors with natural curved tips, should be placed at a slant.

≫ Arrange sunflowers with large flower heads nodding over the sides and larger ones at the base.

≫ Yellow dahlias go in center for fill.

≫ Plumelike goldenrod from the fields adds texture and unity.

How-To

UNITY

Plant material: tuberoses, naked lady, lisianthus, bachelor buttons, asters, and veron

≫ The key to this arrangement in a narrow neck opening is to use thin stems of plant material.

≫ Strip foliage to allow use of a variety of flowers, color, and texture.

≫ Fragrant stems of white tuberoses form the top.

≫ Slender stems of naked lady with pale pink blossoms (they have no foliage) are added to enhance the vertical line.

≫ Asters of complementary colors, brought forward and down at base, fill the vertical space.

≫ Graceful furled blooms of pale pink lisianthus should be placed off to the sides.

≫ Blue bachelor buttons slightly expand the design.

≫ Blue veronica placed with the curved stems adds interest and unity, carrying out the flow of design.

POPPIES

Plant material: red hot poker, poppies, forsythia, and dried curls of pampas grass

≫ One stem of red hot poker is placed at the top to give height and focus.

≫ Various colors of poppies should be arranged with several facing forward and others facing the sides.

≫ Several stems of yellow forsythia fill in to break up the roundness.

≫ The swirls of dried grasses give a lively and fascinating touch to the arrangement.

Dried Flowers

YULETIDE DRIED-FLOWER TREE

Henry Francis du Pont's love of flowers was the inspiration for the Yuletide dried-flower tree. Color, texture, and the harmonious blending of plant material were the considerations for this tribute to our museum's founder. The response to the first Yuletide tree in 1986 was overwhelming. The tree continues to be a highlight of the annual tour.

To create the "largest bouquet" ever made at Winterthur, we chose a wide variety of flowers and plant material from the Winterthur cutting gardens and fields and used two methods of drying: silica gel and hanging.

SILICA GEL

One method for drying flower heads calls for "flower dri" (silica gel). Silica gel is a desiccant, a substance that has a great affinity for water; it rapidly absorbs moisture from flowers. The white powder has small blue crystals and is reusable indefinitely. As the powder absorbs moisture, the blue crystals turn pink, indicating that they can absorb no more moisture. Simply put silica gel in a 350-degree oven for an hour or so and the crystals will turn blue and be ready for another use.

General considerations with this method of drying:

≫ All flowers should be absolutely fresh.

≫ Dry flowers in several stages of bloom: buds, partially open, fully open, and some with foliage.

≫ Before drying, flowers must be wired since they become fragile once dried.

≫ Put similar types of plant material in the same box.

≫ Flowers shrink when dried and many also darken.

≫ Small, fragile flowers will take two or three days to dry.

≫ Most will take five to seven days.

≫ If the material feels slightly limp, it is not dry. Bury in the gel for several more days.

Dried Flowers

Steps to follow:

≫ Cut off flower heads.

≫ Insert wire through the center of the flower, loop, pull down through the flower head so that the head is secure.

≫ Place two inches flower dri in bottom of pan.

≫ Place flower head "heads up" in flower dri.

≫ Pour flower dri over flower heads and between each layer of petals. Cover completely.

≫ For long stems such as snapdragon and delphinium, place horizontally on flower dri. Cover completely.

≫ Cover and seal flowers in airtight pan.

≫ Mark flower type on pan.

≫ Allow ample time for flowers to dry.

≫ When flowers are dry, remove carefully. Gently pull flower heads up while dusting off flower dri.

≫ Store in covered box.

≫ Mark flower type on box.

Yuletide flowers dried in this manner:

Aster	pink, blue, white	Tends to crumble if too dry.
Black-eyed Susan		Short drying period.
Dahlia	white, yellow, pink, lavender	Cactus type gives great effect.
Delphinium	blue	Use short stems.
Marigold	yellow, orange	Tends to darken while drying.
Narcissus	yellow, white	Tends to wilt easily.
Peony	white, pink	Use small blossoms for best results.
Queen Anne's lace		Very easy to dry.
Rose	all colors	Beautiful. Petals fall easily.
Snapdragons	orange, yellow, pink	Use short stems.
Strawflower		Simple to use. No need to place in flower dri. Cut flower head, wire, and store in box.
Zinnia	all colors	Easy to dry and good color retention.

Dried Flowers

HANGING METHOD

A second method of drying is "hanging" flowers in small bunches until dry.

Yuletide plant material dried in this manner:

Artemesia	gray, spikelike	
Baby's breath	white	Excellent for giving lightness to tree.
Cockscomb	pink, yellow, maroon crest	Great for drying.
Dusty miller	gray	Leaves curl as they dry.
Globe amaranth	pink, white, maroon	Looks like clover. Commonly called "clover flower."
Goldenrod		Wonderful fill. Several species and shapes used; plumelike and clublike.
Hydrangea	H. paniculata 'Grandiflora' "Pee Gee" in tree form	Wait until hydrangea begins to turn pale pink before picking. All size blooms used. Easy to dry.
Lamb's ears	gray, wooly leaves	
Peter's penny	gray	Pennylike shape.
Salvia	blue	Goes from bright blue to pleasant pale blue when dry.
Statice	blue, yellow, white	Easy to dry. Retains color.
Yarrow	yellow	

The 18-foot Yuletide fir tree is first covered with more than 1,000 white lights. Then hundreds of dried flowers and other plant material are carefully placed, decorating from top to the bottom—a process that takes several days.

Dried Flowers

Glossary

Achillea	**Yarrow**	perennial	late spring to early fall

Large, flat-topped clusters of tiny flowers in yellow, white, pink, crimson, or purple with feathery, aromatic foliage.

Alstroemeria	**Peruvian lily**	tuber	spring and summer

Trumpetlike flowers of cream, pink, salmon, orange, yellow, purple, or white on graceful, slender stems. Superb cut flowers, long-lasting.

Anemone coronaria	**Windflower**	perennial	early spring

Daisylike or poppylike flowers in vivid shades of blue, purple, white, pink, and fuchsia.

Antirrhinum	**Snapdragon**	annual	summer

Two-lipped, tubular blossoms arranged on vertical spikes in a wide array of colors: rose, peach, bronze, pinks, whites, and yellows.

Artemesia	**Wormwood**	perennial	late summer

Tall stems of silvery gray aromatic foliage. Leaves of different varieties vary from gray, gray-green, silver-gray, white, light and dark green.

A. stelleriana	**Dusty miller**	perennial	summer and fall

Highly prized for silvery white foliage.

Aruncus	**Goat's beard**	perennial	early summer

Large, feathery plumes of creamy white flowers with *astilbe*-like foliage.

Asclepias tuberosa	**Butterfly weed**	perennial	summer

Orange, waxy flowers with waxy, green leaves.

Aster	**Aster**	annual/perennial	summer and fall

Hundred of species. Flowers look like small daisies with yellow center but with many more petals. Pastel of lavender, blue, pink, rose, and white.

Astilbe	**False spirea**	perennial	summer

Tapering plumes of feathery flowers in a range of colors from pink through mauves to red as well as white and cream on fernlike foliage. Airy accent to mass arrangements.

Belamcanda	**Blackberry lily**	perennial	midsummer

Top performer *(Belamcanda chinensis)* has orange flowers with red spots, but there are hybrids in pink, purple, red, white, and yellow without spots. Flowers fade to green seed capsules of large, round, shiny black seeds that look like a blackberry.

Glossary

Brassica	**Wild mustard**	wildflower	spring

Clusters of small, yellow flowers at the end of branches. Grows freely in fields. Popular "fill."

Calendula officinalis	**Pot-marigold**	annual	summer

Hardy, old-fashioned cottage flowers in bright yellow and orange. Splendid cut flowers.

Celastrus scandens	**Bittersweet**	vine	summer

Fast-growing twining vine prized for its yellow fruit that, when split open, shows clusters of orange-red berries. Effective accent in fall arrangements.

Celosia	**Cockscomb**	annual	late summer

C. argentea cristata - large, wooly, round flower head
C. argentea plumosa - feather, plumed type
Variety of yellows, oranges, reds, and purples. Spectacular, showy flower heads. Interesting accent for arrangements.

Centaurea cyanus	**Bachelor buttons**	annual	summer

A button-type flower in blue, pink, or white. If stem is weak, insert wire to base.

Cercis canadensis	**Redbud**	tree	spring

Clusters of rosy pink flowers on bare branches. Provides a colorful, airy look.

Chaenomeles	**Quince**	deciduous shrub	spring

Waxy, apple-blossom-type flowers on leafless branches. Mainly shades of red but also white, pink, and orange. Good for spring arrangements.

Chrysanthemum	**Chrysanthemum**	perennial	summer to fall

Hundreds of varieties: singles, pompon, spoon, spider with various forms, colors, sizes, and blooming period.

Cleome	**Spider flower**	annual	summer

Big, airy flower clusters. Pink, lavender, or white. Interesting seed pods on stalks.

Consolida	**Larkspur**	annual	spring to midsummer

Tall, beautiful spikes of feathery flowers in shades of blue, salmon, rose, lilac, purple, or white.

Convallaria majalis	**Lily of the valley**	perennial	spring

Fragrant, delicate sprays of white bells on short stems. Lovely for small bouquets.

Glossary

Coreopsis	**Coreopsis**	annual/perennial	spring to summer

Yellow, daisylike flowers on slender, single stalks. Brilliant color and long-lasting.

Cornus florida	**Dogwood**	deciduous tree	spring

White or pink florets in spring. Crimson foliage with berries in fall.

Cortaderia selloana	**Pampas grass**	perennial	summer

Tall, handsome, snowy white plumes. Leaves curl when dry.

Cosmos	**Cosmos**	annual	summer

Tall stems of white, pink, red, and lavender daisylike flowers with foliage.

Dahlia	**Dahlia**	tuber	midsummer

Fleshy, bright flowers with varied shapes and sizes in white, red, mauve, yellow, and orange. Long stems. Excellent and showy.

Daucus carota	**Queen Anne's lace**	wildflower	summer

Flat clusters of lacy, white, tiny flowers with feathery, fernlike leaves.

Delphinium	**Delphinium**	perennial	spring to summer

Tall spires of varying shades of blue flowers. Also white, pink, and purple varieties.

Dendrobium	**Orchid**		florist

Blossoms on long stems in white, fuchsia, and purple. Long-lasting. Good in arrangements.

Deutzia	**Deutzia**	deciduous shrub	spring

Long, slender branches with small clusters of frilled, bell-like flowers in pink or white.

Digitalis	**Foxglove**	biennial/perennial	summer

Tall, stately, graceful spires in white, cream, yellow, pink, lavender, magenta, and purple. Showy.

Eucalyptus	**Eucalyptus**	foliage	florist

Green to gray foliage, some very fragrant.

Euphorbia pulcherrima	**Poinsettia**	tropical shrub	florist

Various shades of reds, pinks, and whites.

Glossary

Eustoma grandiflorum	**Lisianthus**	annual	summer

Unopened blossoms resemble rosebuds; opening flowers are like frilly tulips; fully opened resemble poppies. Pink, white, violet-blue, some with colored ruffled edges. Magnificent cut flowers.

Foeniculum vulgare	**Fennel**	field flower	spring

Yellow-green, wiry stems similar to Queen Anne's lace.

Forsythia	**Forsythia**	deciduous shrub	spring

Bright yellow flowers on long, curving stems.

Freesia	**Freesia**	bulb	spring

One of the most scented of cut flowers. Tubular flowers in white, pink, lavender, and gold.

Gaillardia	**Blanket flower**	annual/perennial	early summer

Daisylike blossoms in red, yellow, orange, or maroon; often banded.

Gerbera	**Transvaal daisy**	perennial	summer

Brightly colored, daisylike flowers in cream, yellow, orange, red, pink, or coral.

Gladiolus	**Gladiolus**	corm	summer

Tall, slightly arching stems of brightly colored flowers. The leaves are long and swordlike. Most colors are available except true blue.

Gomphrena globosa	**Globe amaranth**	annual	summer

Globular flowers of white, yellow, orange, red, pink, and purple. Flower heads resemble those of clover. Delicate accent to bouquets.

Gypsophila	**Baby's breath**	annual/perennial	summer

Marvelous airy plant with fine, wiry stems and little puffs of dainty white or rose-pink flowers.

Hamamelis	**Witch hazel**	shrub	winter

Flowers are made up of clusters of spidery, scented flowers that bloom in the dead of winter.

Helianthus	**Sunflower**	annual/perennial	summer

Tall, daisylike flowers. The annual, *Helianthus annuus,* has a large, dark central disc.

Helichrysum bracteatum	**Strawflower**	annual	summer

Daisylike heads with strawlike pointed petals with yellow, orange-white, or red blooms. Harvest for drying just as they open.

Glossary

Heuchera	**Coral bells**	perennial	spring

Bell-shaped florets of pink, red, coral, or white.

Hydrangea	**Hydrangea**	deciduous shrub	summer

Numerous species and cultivars with large mops of flower heads and others with pointed spikes and delicate lace caps. White, blue, mauve, or pink.

Iris	**Iris**	bulb/rhizome	spring

Iris differ widely in plant, color, and form.
Hybrid Dutch iris: Orchidlike flowers in white, yellow, and blue.
Bearded iris: Many colors. Not long-lasting. Cut when first bud is ready to open.

Ixia	**Izia**	corm	spring

Slender-stemmed bulbous plants with several starlike flowers per stem. Blush to pink.

Kniphofia uvaria	**Redhot poker**	perennial	summer

Dense, bottlebrush spires. Orange-red at top and yellow or yellow-green below.

Lathyrus odoratus	**Sweet pea**	annual	summer

Multiflower stems of delicate, airy blossoms that look like miniature sunbonnets.
Yellow, peach, white, rose, blue, purple, and nearly black on leafless stems.

Liatris spicata	**Liatris**	perennial	summer

Dense spikes of tall purple-rose or white flowers. Blooms from top down.

Ligustrum	**Privet**	shrub	spring

Useful for its foliage. White flowers in spring and black berries in autumn.

Lilium	**Lily**	bulb	summer

Beautiful, well-loved flowers. Large range of colors (except blue), either plain or spotted.

Limonium sinuatum	**Sea lavender, statice**	annual	summer

Clusters of paper-textured blossoms of blue, lavender, rose, or white on many-branched stems.

Lupinus	**Lupine**	annual	summer

Graceful spikes in blue, lavender, pink, yellow, white, or bicolor.
Cut while upper blossoms are still buds.

Lycoris squamigera	**Naked lady**	bulb	summer

Trumpet-shaped lilac-rose flowers that bloom without foliage on slender stems.

Glossary

Lysimachia clethroides	**Loosestrife**	perennial	summer

Tiny, white flowers on thin spikes that arch out.

Lythrum salicaria	**Purple loosestrife**	perennial	summer

Tall, herbaceous plants with spires of brilliant purple flowers.

Macleaya cordata	**Plume poppy**	perennial	summer

Long plumes of feathery, pinkish white flowers.

Magnolia grandiflora	**Magnolia**	evergreen	summer

White flowers with rich fragrance. Green, glossy leaves good for arrangements.

Matthiola incana	**Stock**	annual/biennial	spring to summer

Tall spires of scented flowers in white, ivory, rose, lilac, magenta, and peach.

Molucella laevis	**Bells of Ireland**	annual	summer

Tall stems of green trumpets with tiny white flowers.

Narcissus	**Daffodil**	bulb	spring

Popular spring bulbs with trumpets or cups of petals. Mainly yellow but also white, orange, and pink. Cut just as bud begins to open.

Nerine lily	**Nerine lily**	bulb	florist

Delicate, long-lasting pink trumpetlike flowers on long, leafless stems.

Nicotania	**Flowering tobacco**	annual	summer

Starry flowered plant in a variety of colors, green being the most interesting.

Paeonia	**Peony**	perennial	spring

Large, bold flower heads in white, pinks, to dark purple. Can be single or double.

Papaver	**Poppy**	annual/perennial	late spring

Brightly colored flowers with tissuelike petals. Colors are white, yellow, orange, red, or rose.

Philadelphus	**Mock orange**	deciduous shrub	spring

Hardy shrub with heavily scented white flowers. Branches provide structure in arrangements.

Phlox paniculata	**Phlox**	perennial	spring

Pyramid-shaped balls of compact, showy heads. White, cream, pink, coral, red, lavender, purple.

Glossary

Physostegia virginiana	**False dragonhead**	perennial	midsummer
	Pink or white flowers on narrow spikes.		
Phytolacca americana	**Pokeberry**	wildflower/weed	spring
	Useful and effective when berries are light green. Provides great structure.		
Polianthes tuberosa	**Tuberose**	tuber	summer and fall
	Long stems of powerfully sweet white flowers. A double form called 'Pearl' is more fragrant than single types.		
Prunus	**Prunus**	tree	spring
	Ornamental flowering almond and cherry with weeping forms. Excellent in arrangements.		
Ranunculus asiaticus	**Ranunculus**	bulb	spring
	Brightly colored blooms in white, cream, yellow, orange, red, or pink.		
Rhododendron	**Azalea**	shrub	spring
	Flowering branches in white, yellow, orange, scarlet, rose-pink, purple. Branches form colorful outline for arrangements. Buds open well in water.		
Rosa	**Rose**	deciduous shrub	spring to summer
	Large family of shrubs with a good range of colors.		
Rudbeckia	**Coneflower**	perennial	summer
	Bright yellow or orange daisylike petals with dark brown center. Long, rough stems.		
Rumex	**Dock**	wildflower	fall
	Long, straight, firm reddish brown flower heads. Dries well for fall arrangements.		
Salix caprea	**Pussy willow**	deciduous shrub	late winter
	Variation in bark color during winter, pinkish gray catkins.		
Salvia	**Salvia**	annual	summer
	Tubular blue flowers in branched spikes.		
Scabiosa	**Scabiosa**	annual	summer
	Round-head flowers resembling a pincushion in blue, pink, rose, and salmon.		
Scilla	**Squill**	bulb	spring
	Bell-shaped flowers on tall spikes in blue, white, and pink.		

Glossary

Stachys byzantina	**Lamb's ear**	perennial	spring to late summer
	Soft, felty silver leaves. Produces a wooly, upright stalk with pink to purple flowers on tallish stems. Gray foliage mixes well with flowers.		
Sedum x Autumn Joy	**Autumn joy**	perennial	summer to fall
	Large flower heads. Light pink to salmon that become rosy russet in autumn.		
Solidago	**Goldenrod**	wildflower	summer
	Long-stemmed plants with fluffy, feathery plumes.		
Spiraea	**Bridal wreath**	deciduous shrub	spring
	Sprays of white flowers on arching branches. Gives lightness and movement to arrangements.		
Syringa	**Lilac**	deciduous shrub	spring
	Large clusters of fragrant flowers in white and varying shades of mauve and purple.		
Tagetes	**Marigold**	annual	summer
	Showy, round flower forms in tints of yellow and orange.		
Trachymene coerulea	**Blue lace**	annual	summer
	Tiny sky-blue flowers in sweet-scented clusters resembling umbrellas at top of the stems.		
Tulipa	**Tulip**	bulb	spring
	Brightly colored chalices in a wide range of colors including near-black. Some bicolors.		
Veronica	**Speedwell**	perennial	summer
	Narrow spikes of flowers in white, pink, blue, or purple. Upright stems.		
Viburnum	**Viburnum**	deciduous shrub	spring
	Whitish, fragrant clusters in spring and colorful foliage in fall.		
Zantedeschia	**Calla lily**	corm	summer
	Showy, flaring, trumpetlike flowers in white, cream, yellow, and pink. High style.		
Zinnia	**Zinnia**	annual	summer
	Very colorful in reds, creams, yellows, and even green. Wide variety of heights.		

Glossary